wordsfromtheworm

n unauthorized trip through the mind of dennis rodman

D1665533

compiled by david whitaker

The quotations in this book are reproduced from interviews with Dennis Rodman.

01   00   99   98   97   5   4   3   2   1

Library of Congress Catalog Card Number: 97-72598
International Standard Book Number: 1-56625-0870

Cover and interior design by Augustine Janairo Antenorcruz
Cover photography by Blair Jensen/Visages

Bonus Books, Inc. 160 East Illinois Street, Chicago, Illinois 60611
Printed in the United States of America

contents

introduction

●

If you've come this far, it's already too late. There is no turning back. Like a clumsy ricochet off the front rim, he already has you in his grasp.

This is the psychedelic land of Dennis Rodman, where basketball is a sideshow and Andy Warhol a hairstyle. Check your inhibitions, but not your pumps, at the door.

Our host anxiously awaits you, but before going inside, a few tips. Kicking, biting and head-butting are not permitted by order of the commissioner. That does not mean, however, that this trip will be free of danger. It could get ugly, scary, even a bit strange.

Like a stream that's not sure where it's flowing, Mr. Rodman is a natural resource of exciting contradiction, an eclectic rebel unflushed by comparisons to Elvis Presley, James Dean, Jimi Hendrix and...yes, Ru Paul.

To many, this unapologetic chameleon is a ripe breath of fresh air. To others, a throbbing headache. And to some, a distant heartache.

It is plausible you will enter as one, and return another. Dramatic transformations are not uncommon to this man. His own metamorphosis is difficult to grasp, a prime element of the Rodman mystique.

Inside, we offer no simple answers. In fact, we don't even bother with questions. What lies ahead is an unauthorized compilation of peerless and fearless quotes taken from his many encounters with the press. Serving as court jester to his own public trials and triumphs, Mr. Rodman talks about his mighty rebounding skills, his troubled upbringing, his philosophical approach to life, his flair for women's clothing and much more. We are not responsible for any misplaced values along the way.

While accompanied by media attribution, we warn you each quote is unavoidably taken out of context. The words of Mr. Rodman stand alone, in all his sound-bite hysteria. He's the riddler, and you're the reader. Whether diagnosing, or just digesting, hold on tight because you're calling on a man who claims he was born to be wild.

"Beyond the hair, tattoos and earrings, he's just like you and me." That's what Bob Hill, Mr. Rodman's coach when he was with the San Antonio Spurs, once said of your humble host. But you better judge for yourself. Right this way please...   d a v i d   w h i t a k e r

a **worm** in bulls clothing

before Dennis Rodman was traded to the Chicago Bulls at the start of the 1995-96 season, he had already gained an authentic reputation with NBA fans across the country. His tough-guy flamboyance with the Detroit Pistons solidified his place on the basketball court. His blond ambition with the San Antonio Spurs, which included a brief romance with Madonna, nudged him toward the realm of superstar. But the Rodman makeover wasn't complete until he began running with the Bulls.

"People love to hate Dennis Rodman. But once I'm on your team, people love me."

st. petersburg times.   november 3, 1995

"It's like I'm a Michael Jordan. But **I'm a Michael Jordan on the flip side**."

p e o p l e   w e e k l y .   may 15, 1995

"people have to realize that **this team is going to be like a circus on the road. Without me, it would be a circus and with me, it's even more of a circus**, with Michael [Jordan], scottie [Pippen], me and [Tony] kukoc. A lot of people want to come see the bulls again."

chicago tribune. october 14, 1995

"we have a good relationship. we don't talk at all, but it's a good relationship. **I'll back Scottie, I'll back Michael... once we get on the floor. It's all business**." beckett profiles. 1996

"This is not about making friends. I have enough of those already. otherwise, I don't trust anybody and I don't trust the game, not after the way I've been lied to and screwed around elsewhere. But I can trust me out there for 48 minutes, which is what this is about....That's all it should be about."

chicago tribune. november 3, 1995

"Dennis Rodman is going to be Dennis Rodman. I'm going to play hard, kick [butt] and whatever the league says I'm doing wrong, I'm going to keep on doing it."

st. petersburg times. november 3, 1995

growing up

At the age of 19, Rodman stood a mere 5'9". He had no high school basketball experience behind him and no reason to think he'd ever get a shot at becoming a two-time NBA all-star. Raised by his mother in a Dallas housing project, height wasn't the only obstacle he overcame in his rise to the top. When he was 22, Rodman was offered a scholarship to play at Southeastern Oklahoma University. He continued to grow, and accepted it like a gift.

"I think there's 20 years of my life that has passed me by totally. And now I have brought it back in time, trying to find out what I've wanted to do all my life. And **I think I'm exploring all the possibilities now**."

rolling stone.   december 12, 1996

"**I was just doing nothing**, being a lowlife." **p e o p l e   w e e k l y .**   may 15, 1995

[after dropping out for academic reasons after
14 games with Cooke County College in Texas]
**"The way I was going I would've
ended up in jail for sure**. My mother
gave me money to look for a job, but I would take it
and just go hang out. Finally she told me she was
sick and tired of me sitting around the house bum-
ming, so she threw me out."

sports illustrated.   may 2, 1988

[On getting taller] "…it's like someone just came to the front door and said, 'Here — there's a gift, right there. open it up. **Here's a brand-new life if you want it**.'"

rolling stone. december 12, 1996

'bound for **glory**

Strip away the glitzy sex appeal and marketing madness that's hooked the MTV generation, and you have one of the greatest rebounders the game has ever seen. He's not the tallest guy out there, nor the greatest leaper. But, somehow, he always seems to find the ball. Is it the shoes? Nope. It's his tireless determination. He not only loves to win, he expects to win.

"A lot of people think I'm dumb or stupid and that I am not a coachable person. They're going to realize that Dennis Rodman is a lot smarter than they give him credit for. I know the offense inside and out. I act like I'm stupid in practice, 'where should I go?' when I get in the game, I fit right on in."

chicago tribune. october 14, 1995

"The one thing that they cannot take away from me is that **I am a competitor, a fighter, and I go out there and work my butt off every night.** And rebounding is how I express myself."

beckett profiles. 1996

"**I'm the black Bill Laimbeer** of the '90s." **chicago tribune.** january 22, 1996

"people think I just go get the damn ball, because they don't take the time to really look at what I do. **Rebounding isn't brain surgery, but there's more to it than being able to jump higher than the next guy**. A lot of the work is done before you ever even jump."

sports illustrated. october 23, 1995

"I'm surprised that I can even get to the ball compared to most guys who are 6-10 and 7 feet tall. Especially when **I've got guys grabbing me and holding me and doing all kinds of things to keep me away from the ball**. They don't even know me well enough to be doing some of the things they do."

chicago tribune. february 29, 1996

"I just try to predict where the ball is going to be and just be in that spot." beckett profiles. 1996 "since i've been in this league for 10 years, **I've gotten a knack for knowing where the ball is going to go when a guy is shooting**. i told these guys before the season that once i know about everybody on this team — where they like to shoot the ball and when to shoot — i'll know how to get into position to try and get the ball."

chicago tribune. february 29, 1996

"I know shooters, but that's not enough. You have to watch the flight of the ball. Most guys see the shot go up and they turn and look at the rim, waiting for the ball to come off. **I watch the ball in the air and make an adjustment if I need to.**"

s p o r t s   i l l u s t r a t e d .   october 23, 1995

"There's nothing else on my mind other than winning. **Once I'm on that court, I have the feeling like I'm born to be wild**, born to be free..."

i n t e r v i e w .   february 1997

"No one can ever say, 'we compare Dennis to...' who? No one can compare me to anybody.... They say, Wilt Chamberlain. Well, he was 7-foot-4. Bill Russell? He had a beard. Nobody. I don't want to be compared to anybody. **I just want to be known as Dennis Rodman, the person that went out there and gave 110 percent every night.**" beckett profiles. 1996

down in detroit

not everything was champagne and champion-ships when Rodman was with the Detroit Pistons — especially when coach Chuck Daly, who was a father figure to him, left the team. Rodman has not only rebounded from bouts of depression, he's reinvented himself. Still, basketball's clowned prince claims he's haunted by dreams of death.

"I dream about death all the time, just because I know it's coming some day, and for some reason I've got to figure out which way to go, how it's gonna happen. It's a weird feeling. You name every way in the world, I've thought of all of them."

rolling stone. december 12, 1996

"I woke up one day and said to myself, hey, my life has been a big cycle. one month I'm bleeding to death, one month I'm in a psycho zone. Then, **all of a sudden, the cycles were in balance**."

sports illustrated. may 29, 1995

"one day i woke up, drove my truck to the woods and just sat there wondering what the hell i was gonna do besides basketball. And all of a sudden i started to project this image....yea or nay. if you're gonna do it, do it. if you ain't gonna do it, just stay as you are and be the same Dennis Rodman you were in Detroit. suddenly, i said, 'Hell with it,' and broke away. i tried something bold. **I created something that everyone has been afraid of: the entertainer, the Dennis Rodman I was born to be**." **playboy.** january 1996

"sometimes ı say ı'm going to play
basketball and go-go-go until ı drop dead.
**I'm not afraid of dying at all.
It's just the next boundary.**"

s p o r t s   i l l u s t r a t e d .   may 29, 1995

the **kick**

more than his ferocious rebounding, rebellious tattoos, two-toned hairdo or spirited chatter, Rodman's 1996-97 season may be looked back on as the year of "The Kick." Not only did his sneakered swipe — at a photographer who inadvertently tripped him — result in a whopping 11-game suspension and a hefty out-of-court settlement with the victim in question, it prompted an unrivaled media event that included counsel from Rev. Jesse Jackson, comments from President Clinton, a high-profile interview on ABC-TV and a flashy appearance on NBC's "The Tonight Show". Promising to donate his paycheck for the first eleven games back after his suspension, Rodman soon wormed his way back into the favor of Bulls fans. But not everyone was as forgiving, including some former NBA stars.

"I didn't kick him in the groin....
**If that's his groin, his wife
must really love him**."

ABC-TV's primetime live. january 22, 1997

"It was a bad thing on my part...but it's a sorry thing when the first thing we have to say when something goes bad is, 'I wanna sue you.' But **I'm paying the price for being me**..."

the tonight show. february 6, 1997

"I don't need help. if they want me to see a counselor, i'll see him. we'll play cards."

chicago sun-times. january 23, 1997

"A few of those guys said, 'kick his butt out.' They're just bitter because their time has passed....**If you don't want to stick behind me, don't say nothin' about me at all**. My goal is to win a championship. I guess if I do that, people are going to love me again. If I do something wrong, people are going to hate me."

the associated press. february 12, 1997

"I paid the guy $200,000 because I kicked him and I turn around and he's been to jail for beating his girlfriend....what would be a bigger story: me beating my wife or girlfriend or me kicking a photographer? you make the call. i think he should give the money to charity or come and shake my hand and apologize to me for taking me for $200,000."

chicago tribune. february 9, 1997

"I'm not crazy, I know exactly what's going on....people have problems. It's a part of life."

ABC-TV's primetime live. january 22, 1997

[After tumbling into another photographer in his first game back from the suspension] **"It would have been a classic if I kissed him**. But he probably would have sued me for slobbering all over him."

the associated press. february 12, 1997

"I've just showed that professional athletes are not flawless. We make mistakes. we have breakdowns. we are emotional. we are kids inside. we're everything that you are. so don't treat us like we're gods and put us on a pedestal."

i n t e r v i e w.   february 1997

building a rep'

While revered by many and reviled by some, Rodman's true identity, his lasting reputation, remains elusive. He's seen as both sex symbol and jerk, leader and outcast, father and freak. He's had his scrapes with league officials, coaches, the media, opposing players and even his own teammates. And he's certainly not shy in sharing — even showing — his alternative lifestyle. Whether in shorts or a gown, Rodman's an open book. Easy reading, he's not.

"They say Elvis is dead. He's not dead. He's just a different color. he's 6 ft. 8 in., 225 pounds, plays basketball, and he's black." **t i m e .** february 24, 1997

"I totally feel like a rock star more than a basketball player. I totally think: Have I got to go and play basketball now?" **rolling stone.** december 12, 1996

"I don't get paid 9 million dollars just to look good. **I'm an entertainer**."

A B C - T V ' s   p r i m e t i m e   l i v e .   january 22, 1997

"The Dennis Rodman system is to go out there and kick somebody's ass. **Live your life to the fullest — that's the way Dennis Rodman lives**. That's his rule. That's my rule. I want to live life the way life should be lived." **playboy.** january 1996

"I don't give a damn what people think of Dennis Rodman, because people don't know Dennis Rodman."

G.Q.   january 1995

"This is what I am. I don't try to be a big, big role model for kids. But **kids look at me as independent and happy and free and I love what I'm doing**. That is more of a role model than anything."

beckett profiles. 1996

"I dress to please Dennis Rodman.
**When I feel good, I dress good.
When I feel bad, I dress good.**"

larry king live on CNN.   march 28, 1997

"I go [shopping] by myself. **This is me, baby. What you see is what you get**." the tonight show. february 6, 1997

"people try to embed this certain image in me and make me believe it. It pisses me off and makes me an even more enraged person than I am. I want to think the way Dennis Rodman thinks. That's why **God put you on this earth, to be an individual person — not to be the same as some other person**." G.Q. february 1997

"...**I don't want and I don't need to step into that plastic image that all the NBA players except for me represent**. I'm being real. I play my own fiddle and my own drum, but I also go out there and bust my ass and do what I have to do to win." **interview.** november 1995

"I have a lot of gay friends, and they kiss me and stuff — you know, friendly kisses. Like when you go to italy or france, they kiss you on the cheek. it's no big deal." **i n s i d e s p o r t s .** february 1996

"I feel more like Dennis [in women's clothing]. It makes me feel beautiful and more confident. It makes me feel that people are gonna accept me no matter what I am. It makes me feel that I'm fulfilling every possibility of what life has to offer me." **the advocate.** january 21, 1997

"...everybody visualizes being gay - they think, should I do it or not? The reason they can't is because they think it's unethical. They think it's a sin. Hell, **you're not bad if you're gay, and it doesn't make you any less of a person**."

sports illustrated. may 29, 1995

"...All I'm doing is challenging the world when I say, 'Hey, one day I may be gay. Or maybe I am gay and I'm just not accepting the fact or it hasn't hit me yet. So **accept me for who I am — gay or straight. Either way, I'm going to be the same Dennis Rodman**." the advocate. january 21, 1997

the **actor** bares all ●

It's finally happened, Dennis Rodman can be seen at a theater near you. With friends like Pearl Jam's Eddie Vedder and the Material Girl, could an album be far behind? And what about basketball?

While it's commonly known he dreams of playing his final NBA game in the nude, it's unlikely the Worm will ever streak into quiet retirement. In a nation addicted to the distraction of sports, Dennis Rodman has become the distraction. He leaves them wanting more and wonders when they'll get enough...or, when he'll get enough.

"...I'm very emotional and very high-strung about certain things, but when you've been tested and pushed so much in every game, it's hard to hold back."

the associated press. 1996

"I know people are getting sick and tired of Dennis Rodman. You have your time, and then you move on. I want people to look at me not just as an athlete; I want them to think of me as a universal person. **Dennis Rodman's a multi-talented, individual person**. I think my next forte will be doing movies."

G.Q. january 1995

"if these acting things work out, and if I have other offers, I'm going to say, 'The hell with basketball.'" beckett profiles. 1996

"I will be in show business, but **I'm not going to play some weak-ass basketball player**. That would be stupid."

s p o r t s   i l l u s t r a t e d .   may 29, 1995

"...I want a role that's more challenging.
**I'll go on the damned TV like
I've been there all my life**.
Action movies. I'd rather be the bad guy."

p l a y b o y . january 1996

"...**don't put me in a lead role**
unless ı have that capability to take a movie from
start to finish." **C B S   c h a n n e l   t w o
c h i c a g o .**   february 26, 1997

"I can see myself with the Lakers for sure...if I don't go back to chicago. I would love to stay in chicago. The people have been great to me."

larry king live on CNN. march 28, 1997

"it's like dying — I'm not afraid of that. If I don't come back [to the Bulls], I don't come back. I can't kiss everybody's (butt) and try to make them like me, 'Hey, I'm a good boy, everybody jump on my good ship Lollipop.' **I just have to do my job and hope people accept that**."

chicago tribune. february 17, 1997

[On playing naked] "That will give me the sense of freedom, the sense of knowing that **I've fulfilled my goal, my destiny**."

rolling stone. december 12, 1996

"Right now **I have to keep striving, striving, striving to be satisfied**: just looking for that one element that's going to keep me happy at all times." **rolling stone.**

december 12, 1996

"Everybody wants a piece of Dennis Rodman. so I got to take advantage of the opportunity while it's here. But I can't be in a hurry. I got to give them a little bit at a time, just enough to keep them wanting more. They shouldn't worry. There's enough of Dennis Rodman to go around." **sport.** april 1997